THE SENSE OF WONDER

RACHEL CARSON

PHOTOGRAPHS BY NICK KELSH

Introduction by Linda Lear

Design by Lia A. Calhoun at Kelsh Wilson *design inc.*

HarperCollins*Publishers*

A previous edition of this book was published in 1965
by Harper & Row Publishers.

Printed in Italy.
For information address HarperCollins Publishers, Inc.,
10 East 53rd Street, New York, NY 10022.

HarperCollins books may be purchased for educational, business, or sales promotional use.
For information please write: Special Markets Department, HarperCollins Publishers, Inc.,
10 East 53rd Street, New York, NY 10022.

The pictures of people in this book do not represent and are not meant to represent
the author or her grandnephew.

THE SENSE OF WONDER first appeared in *Woman's Home Companion*
under the title HELP YOUR CHILD TO WONDER.

FIRST EDITION
Designed by Lia A. Calhoun at Kelsh Wilson *design inc.*
Library of Congress Cataloging-in-Publication Data
ISBN 0-06-757520-X
03 / NI 10 9 8 7 6 5

Rachel Carson intended to expand *The Sense of Wonder*

but time ran out before she could. She also intended a dedication, and so:

This book is for Roger

· 7

For Cotten —NK

Introduction

L I N D A   L E A R

T*he Sense of Wonder* is Rachel Carson's gift to the remembered child in all of us. In these brief pages she captures the essence of the wonder-filled world of children and stirs in us that ancient longing for unity with the living world. The delight she brought to the process of discovery distinguishes all her writing and places her in the pantheon of the greatest nature writers in the English language. In the lyric prose that was her signature, Carson here shares her prescription on how to nurture a lifelong sense of wonder, how to maintain the freshness with which we saw the natural world for the first time, and how to preserve awe and wonder in lives lived so often in opposition to nature. ✎ This essay, first published in July 1956 in *Woman's Home Companion* under the title "Help Your Child to Wonder," reminds us that the child intuitively apprehends the truth that most adults have forgotten—that we are all part of the natural world. Remembering that her perceptive eye for the wonders of nature was sharpened in childhood in company with her mother, Carson counsels that a child needs at least one adult with whom to share the experience, but cautions the adult to adopt the child's attitude. Nature is the arena of shared enjoyment, an equalizer in the adventure of discovery. Carson urges us to explore nature with feelings and emotions, to use all our senses, and to abandon the impulse to teach or explain. Arouse the emotions, Carson admonishes, for the foundation of learning is in what we love.

· 9

Photo of Rachel Carson by Erich Hartmann, Magnum Studios. This, Carson's favorite photo of herself, was taken near her Maine home in the summer of 1960.

One of the distinguishing features of *The Sense of Wonder* is its unexpected nocturnal theme. Carson loved the vast serenity of night and the mystery of nocturnal space and sound, but nowhere so much as on her rocky beach in Maine. There she deepened her own spiritual understanding of the tenacity of life. The adventures she suggests in *The Sense of Wonder* are those she had taken alone at night. But when in the company of a small child or a cherished companion, the rewards were multiplied. Ultimately Carson believed that the value of contemplating the awe and beauty of nature was in spiritual renewal, inner healing, and a new depth to the adventure of humanity. Rachel Carson began work on this essay shortly after her remarkable book on the symbiosis of sea and shore, *The Edge of the Sea*, was published in 1955, and several years before she embarked upon the project that would become *Silent Spring*. She saw in the subject an opportunity "to say in different ways some of the things I want to say before I lay down my pen." Roger Christie, Carson's three year old grandnephew, had visited her in Maine with his mother that summer, and together they explored the woods and tide pools that surrounded her cottage. Roger delighted his aunt with his imaginative response to their common adventures. Many of the activities Carson describes were shared with Roger, some were in the company of her dearest friend, Dorothy Freeman, others were drawn from solitary exploration. Carson's literary agent first urged her to write the essay as a way of getting her to talk about herself. The published article was so well received that Carson decided to expand it into a book. She spent much of the summer of 1959 collecting vignettes from her field notes, and thinking about other experiences she wanted to include.

The "material comes to my door without my half trying" she wrote, but in 1962 the pesticide

controversy created by *Silent Spring* overwhelmed her energies, and *The Sense of Wonder* was

published posthumously in 1965 without further augmentation. ✿ The book you hold

in your hands is the book that Rachel Carson wanted most to complete in her brief life.

"I want very much to do the Wonder book," she wrote shortly before her death, "that would

be Heaven to achieve." She cared passionately about the subject of how to maintain a sense

of wonder and believed the war was won or lost in childhood. She hoped her book would

inspire adults and children alike to experience the sensory and emotional in nature, and

knew that if they did, they would have less appetite for those activities that threatened the

living world. ✿ This new edition of *The Sense of Wonder* includes precisely the kind of

photographs Carson had wanted to accompany her text. "We plan for it to be rather lavishly

illustrated with the most beautiful photographs we can find, some color and some black and

white," she told a friend. Carson wished there might be a good fairy to give to each child

"a sense of wonder so indestructible that it would last throughout life." Sadly Rachel Carson

never met Nick Kelsh or saw his photographs, but they are companions of the spirit. This

partnership of prose and picture embellishes Carson's message as she had hoped and

encourages the work of that good fairy.

Linda Lear
Bethesda, Maryland
Fall 1997

One stormy autumn night when my nephew Roger was about twenty months old I wrapped him in a blanket and carried him down to the beach in the rainy darkness. Out there, just at the edge of where-we-couldn't-see, big waves were thundering in, dimly seen white shapes that boomed and shouted and threw great handfuls of froth at us. Together we laughed for pure joy—he a baby meeting for the first time the wild tumult of Oceanus, I with the salt of half a lifetime of sea love in me. But I think we felt the same spine-tingling response to the vast, roaring ocean and the wild night around us.

A night or two later the storm had blown itself out and I took

Roger again to the beach, this time to carry him along the water's

edge, piercing the darkness with the yellow cone of our flashlight.

Although there was no rain the night was again noisy with breaking

waves and the insistent wind. It was clearly a time and place where

great and elemental things prevailed.

Our adventure on this particular night had to do with life, for

we were searching for ghost crabs, those sand-colored, fleet-legged

beings which Roger had sometimes glimpsed briefly on the beaches

in daytime. But the crabs are chiefly nocturnal, and when not roam-

ing the night beaches they dig little pits near the surf line where they

hide, seemingly watching and waiting for what the sea may bring

them. For me the sight of these small living creatures, solitary and

fragile against the brute force of the sea, had moving philosophic overtones, and I do not pretend that Roger and I reacted with similar

emotions. But it was good to see his infant acceptance of a world of

elemental things, fearing neither the song of the wind nor the dark-

ness nor the roaring surf, entering with baby excitement into the

search for a "ghos."

It was hardly a conventional way to entertain one so young,   · 17

I suppose, but now, with Roger a little past his fourth birthday, we are

continuing that sharing of adventures in the world of nature that we

began in his babyhood, and I think the results are good. The sharing

includes nature in storm as well as calm, by night as well as day, and

is based on having fun together rather than on teaching.

I spend the summer months on the coast of Maine, where I have my own shoreline and my own small tract of woodland. Bayberry and juniper and huckleberry begin at the very edge of the granite rim of shore, and where the land slopes upward from the bay in a wooded knoll the air becomes fragrant with spruce and balsam. Underfoot there is the multi-patterned northern ground cover of blueberry, checkerberry, reindeer moss and bunchberry, and on a hillside of many spruces, with shaded ferny dells and rocky outcroppings—called the Wildwoods—there are lady's-slippers and wood lilies and the slender wands of clintonia with its deep blue berries.

When Roger has visited me in Maine and we have walked

in these woods I have made no conscious effort to name plants or

animals nor to explain to him, but have just expressed my own

pleasure in what we see, calling his attention to this or that but only

as I would share discoveries with an older person. Later I have been

amazed at the way names stick in his mind, for when I show color

slides of my woods plants it is Roger who can identify them. "Oh,

that's what Rachel likes—that's bunchberry!" Or, "That's Jumer

(juniper) but you can't eat those green berries—they are for the

squirrels." I am sure no amount of drill would have implanted the

names so firmly as just going through the woods in the spirit of two

friends on an expedition of exciting discovery.

...drink in the beauty and wonder

at the meaning of what you see.

*I*n the same way Roger learned the shells on my little triangle
of sand that passes for a beach in rocky Maine. When he was
only a year and a half old, they became known to him as winkies
(periwinkles), weks (whelks) and mukkies (mussels) without my
knowing quite how this came about, for I had not tried to teach him.

We have let Roger share our enjoyment of things people
ordinarily deny children because they are inconvenient, interfering
with bedtime, or involving wet clothing that has to be changed or
mud that has to be cleaned off the rug. We have let him join us in
the dark living room before the big picture window to watch the
full moon riding lower and lower toward the far shore of the bay,
setting all the water ablaze with silver flames and finding a thousand
diamonds in the rocks on the shore as the light strikes the flakes
of mica embedded in them. I think we have felt that the memory of
such a scene, photographed year after year by his child's mind,

would mean more to him in manhood than the sleep he was losing.

He told me it would, in his own way, when we had a full moon the

night after his arrival last summer. He sat quietly on my lap for some

time, watching the moon and the water and all the night sky, and

then he whispered, "I'm glad we came."

A rainy day is the perfect time for a walk in the woods.

I always thought so myself; the Maine woods never seem

so fresh and alive as in wet weather. Then all the needles on the

evergreens wear a sheath of silver; ferns seem to have grown to

almost tropical lushness and every leaf has its edging of crystal drops.

Strangely colored fungi—mustard-yellow and apricot and scarlet—

are pushing out of the leaf mold and all the lichens and the mosses

have come alive with green and silver freshness.

Now I know that for children, too, nature reserves some of

her choice rewards for days when her mood may appear to be somber.

Roger reminded me of it on a long walk through rain-drenched

woods last summer—not in words, of course, but by his responses.

There had been rain and fog for days, rain beating on the big picture

window, fog almost shutting out sight of the bay. No lobstermen

coming in to tend their traps, no gulls on the shore, scarcely even a

squirrel to watch. The cottage was fast becoming too small for a

restless three-year-old.

"Let's go for a walk in the woods," I said. "Maybe we'll see a fox

or a deer." So into yellow oilskin coat and sou'wester and outside in

joyous anticipation.

There is something infinitely healing

in the repeated refrains of nature—

the assurance that dawn comes after night,

and spring after the winter.

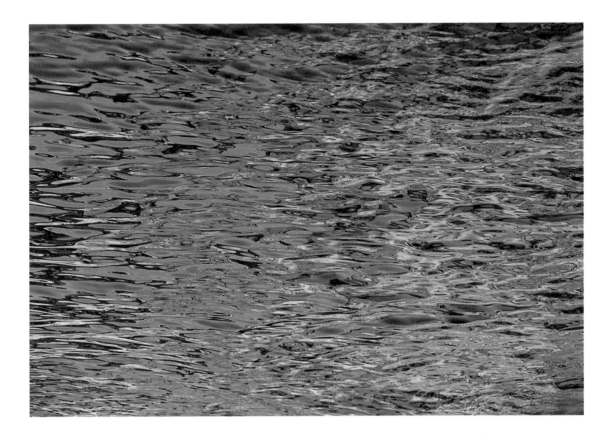

Having always loved the lichens because they have a quality of fairyland—silver rings on a stone, odd little forms like bones or horns or the shell of a sea creature—I was glad to find Roger noticing and responding to the magic change in their appearance wrought by the rain. The woods path was carpeted with the so-called reindeer moss, in reality a lichen. Like an old-fashioned hall runner, it made a narrow strip of silvery gray through the green of the woods, here and there spreading out to cover a larger area. In dry weather the lichen carpet seems thin; it is brittle and crumbles underfoot. Now, saturated with rain which it absorbs like a sponge, it was deep and springy. Roger delighted in its texture, getting down on chubby knees to feel it, and running from one patch to another to jump up and down in the deep, resilient carpet with squeals of pleasure.

It was here that we first played our Christmas tree game. There is a fine crop of young spruces coming along and one can find seedlings of almost any size down to the length of Roger's finger. I began to point out the baby trees.

"This one must be a Christmas tree for the squirrels," I would say. "It's just the right height. On Christmas Eve the red squirrels come and hang little shells and cones and silver threads of lichen on it for ornaments, and then the snow falls and covers it with shining stars, and in the morning the squirrels have a beautiful Christmas tree... And this one is even tinier—it must be for little bugs of some kind—and maybe this bigger one is for the rabbits or woodchucks."

Once this game was started it had to be played on all woods walks, which from now on were punctuated by shouts of, "Don't step on the Christmas tree!"

Many children...

delight in the small and inconspicuous.

A child's world is fresh and new and beautiful, full of wonder and excitement. It is our misfortune that for most of us that clear-eyed vision, that true instinct for what is beautiful and awe-inspiring, is dimmed and even lost before we reach adulthood. If I had influence with the good fairy who is supposed to preside over the christening of all children I should ask that her gift to each child in the world be a sense of wonder so indestructible that it would last throughout life, as an unfailing antidote against the boredom and disenchantments of later years, the sterile preoccupation with things that are artificial, the alienation from the sources of our strength.

54 ·

If a child is to keep alive his inborn sense of wonder without any such gift from the fairies, he needs the companionship of at least one adult who can share it, rediscovering with him the joy, excitement and mystery of the world we live in. Parents often have a sense of inadequacy when confronted on the one hand with the eager, sensitive mind of a child and on the other with a world of complex physical nature, inhabited by a life so various and unfamiliar that it seems hopeless to reduce it to order and knowledge. In a mood of self-defeat, they exclaim, "How can I possibly teach my child about nature—why, I don't even know one bird from another!"

56 ·

I sincerely believe that for the child, and for the parent seek-
ing to guide him, it is not half so important to *know* as to *feel.* If
facts are the seeds that later produce knowledge and wisdom, then
the emotions and the impressions of the senses are the fertile soil in
which the seeds must grow. The years of early childhood are the time
to prepare the soil. Once the emotions have been aroused—a sense of
the beautiful, the excitement of the new and the unknown, a feeling
of sympathy, pity, admiration or love—then we wish for knowledge
about the object of our emotional response. Once found, it has lasting
meaning. It is more important to pave the way for the child to want to
know than to put him on a diet of facts he is not ready to assimilate.

it is not half so important to know as to feel.

*I*f you are a parent who feels he has little nature lore at his disposal there is still much you can do for your child. With him, wherever you are and whatever your resources, you can still look up at the sky—its dawn and twilight beauties, its moving clouds, its stars by night. You can listen to the wind, whether it blows with majestic voice through a forest or sings a many-voiced chorus around the eaves of your house or the corners of your apartment building, and in the listening, you can gain magical release for your thoughts. You can still feel the rain on your face and think of its long journey, its many transmutations, from sea to air to earth. Even if you are a city dweller, you can find some place, perhaps a park or a golf course, where you can observe the mysterious migrations of the birds and the changing seasons. And with your child you can ponder the mystery of a growing seed, even if it be only one planted in a pot of earth in the kitchen window.

Exploring nature with your child is largely a matter of becoming receptive to what lies all around you. It is learning again to use your eyes, ears, nostrils and finger tips, opening up the disused channels of sensory impression.

For most of us, knowledge of our world comes largely through sight, yet we look about with such unseeing eyes that we are partially blind. One way to open your eyes to unnoticed beauty is to ask yourself, "What if I had never seen this before? What if I knew I would never see it again?"

I remember a summer night when such a thought came to me strongly. It was a clear night without a moon. With a friend, I went out on a flat headland that is almost a tiny island, being all but surrounded by the waters of the bay. There the horizons are remote and distant rims on the edge of space. We lay and looked up at the sky and the millions of stars that blazed in darkness. The night was so still that we could hear the buoy on the ledges out beyond the

mouth of the bay. Once or twice a word spoken by someone on the

far shore was carried across on the clear air. A few lights burned in

cottages. Otherwise there was no reminder of other human life;

my companion and I were alone with the stars. I have never seen

them more beautiful: the misty river of the Milky Way flowing across

the sky, the patterns of the constellations standing out bright and

clear, a blazing planet low on the horizon. Once or twice a meteor

burned its way into the earth's atmosphere.

It occurred to me that if this were a sight that could be seen

only once in a century or even once in a human generation, this

little headland would be thronged with spectators. But it can be seen many scores of nights in any year, and so the lights burned

in the cottages and the inhabitants probably gave not a thought to

the beauty overhead; and because they could see it almost any night

perhaps they will never see it.

An experience like that, when one's thoughts are released   · 69

to roam through the lonely spaces of the universe, can be shared

with a child even if you don't know the name of a single star. You

can still drink in the beauty, and think and wonder at the meaning

of what you see.

And then there is the world of little things, seen all too seldom. Many children, perhaps because they themselves are small and closer to the ground than we, notice and delight in the small and inconspicuous. With this beginning, it is easy to share with them the beauties we usually miss because we look too hastily, seeing the whole and not its parts. Some of nature's most exquisite handiwork is on a miniature scale, as anyone knows who has applied a magnifying glass to a snowflake.

An investment of a few dollars in a good hand lens or magnifying glass will bring a new world into being. With your child, look at objects you take for granted as commonplace or uninteresting. A sprinkling of sand grains may appear as gleaming jewels of rose or crystal hue, or as glittering jet beads, or as a mélange of Lilliputian rocks, spines of sea urchins and bits of snail shells.

A lens-aided view into a patch of moss reveals a dense

tropical jungle, in which insects large as tigers prowl amid strangely

formed, luxuriant trees. A bit of pond weed or seaweed put in a glass

container and studied under a lens is found to be populated by

hordes of strange beings, whose activities can entertain you for hours.

Flowers (especially the composites), the early buds of leaf or flower

from any tree, or any small creature reveal unexpected beauty and

complexity when, aided by a lens, we can escape the limitations of

the human size scale.

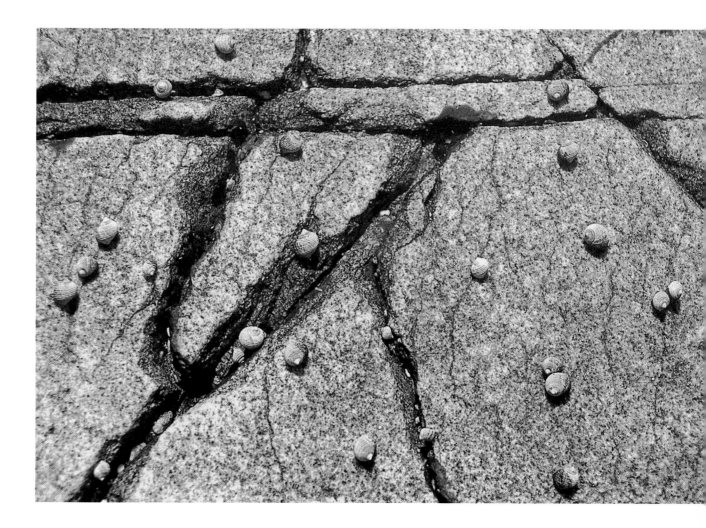

Senses other than sight can prove avenues of delight and

discovery, storing up for us memories and impressions.

Already Roger and I, out early in the morning, have enjoyed the

sharp, clean smell of wood smoke coming from the cottage chimney.

Down on the shore we have savored the smell of low tide—that

marvelous evocation combined of many separate odors, of the world

of seaweeds and fishes and creatures of bizarre shape and habit,

of tides rising and falling on their appointed schedule, of exposed

mud flats and salt rime drying on the rocks. I hope Roger will later

experience, as I do, the rush of remembered delight that comes with

the first breath of that scent, drawn into one's nostrils as one returns

to the sea after a long absence. For the sense of smell, almost more

than any other, has the power to recall memories and it is a pity that

we use it so little.

Hearing can be a source of even more exquisite pleasure but it requires conscious cultivation. I have had people tell me they had never heard the song of a wood thrush, although I knew the bell-like phrases of this bird had been ringing in their back yards every spring. By suggestion and example, I believe children can be helped to hear the many voices about them. Take time to listen and talk about the voices of the earth and what they mean—the majestic voice of thunder, the winds, the sound of surf or flowing streams.

And the voices of living things: No child should grow up

unaware of the dawn chorus of the birds in spring. He will never forget

the experience of a specially planned early rising and going out in the

predawn darkness. The first voices are heard before daybreak. It is

easy to pick out these first, solitary singers. Perhaps a few cardinals are

uttering their clear, rising whistles, like someone calling a dog. Then

the song of a whitethroat, pure and ethereal, with the dreamy quality

of remembered joy. Off in some distant patch of woods a whippoorwill

continues his monotonous night chant, rhythmic and insistent, sound

that is felt almost more than heard. Robins, thrushes, song sparrows,

jays, vireos add their voices. The chorus picks up volume as more and

more robins join in, contributing a fierce rhythm of their own that

soon becomes dominant in the wild medley of voices. In that dawn

chorus one hears the throb of life itself.

Those who contemplate the beauty of the earth

find reserves of strength that will endure

as long as life lasts.

There is other living music. I have already promised Roger that we'll take our flashlights this fall and go out into the garden to hunt for the insects that play little fiddles in the grass and among the shrubbery and flower borders. The sound of the insect orchestra swells and throbs night after night, from midsummer until autumn ends and the frosty nights make the tiny players stiff and numb, and finally the last note is stilled in the long cold. An hour of hunting out the small musicians by flashlight is an adventure any child would love. It gives him a sense of the night's mystery and beauty, and of how alive it is with watchful eyes and little, waiting forms.

The game is to listen, not so much to the full orchestra as to the separate instruments, and to try to locate the players. Perhaps you are drawn, step by step, to a bush from which comes a sweet, high-pitched, endlessly repeated trill. Finally you trace it to a little creature of palest green, with wings as white and insubstantial as moonlight. Or from somewhere along the garden path comes a cheerful, rhythmic chirping, a sound as companionable and homely as a fire crackling on a hearth or a cat's purr. Shifting your light downward you find a black mole cricket disappearing into his grassy den.

Most haunting of all is one I call the fairy bell ringer. I have never found him. I'm not sure I want to. His voice—and surely he himself—are so ethereal, so delicate, so otherworldly, that he should remain invisible, as he has through all the nights I have searched for him. It is exactly the sound that should come from a bell held in the hand of the tiniest elf, inexpressibly clear and silvery, so faint, so barely-to-be-heard that you hold your breath as you bend closer to the green glades from which the fairy chiming comes.

The night is a time, too, to listen for other voices, the calls of bird migrants hurrying northward in spring and southward in autumn. Take your child out on a still October night when there is

little wind and find a quiet place away from traffic noises. Then stand

very still and listen, projecting your consciousness up into the dark

arch of the sky above you. Presently your ears will detect tiny wisps of

sound—sharp chirps, sibilant lisps and call notes. They are the voices

of bird migrants, apparently keeping in touch by their calls with

others of their kind scattered through the sky. I never hear these calls

without a wave of feeling that is compounded of many emotions—a

sense of lonely distances, a compassionate awareness of small lives

controlled and directed by forces beyond volition or denial, a surging

wonder at the sure instinct for route and direction that so far has

baffled human efforts to explain it.

If the moon is full and the night skies are alive with the calls

of bird migrants, then the way is open for another adventure with

your child, if he is old enough to use a telescope or a good pair of binoculars. The sport of watching migrating birds pass across the face

of the moon has become popular and even scientifically important in

recent years, and it is as good a way as I know to give an older child a

sense of the mystery of migration.

Seat yourself comfortably and focus your glass on the moon.

You must learn patience, for unless you are on a well-traveled high-

way of migration you may have to wait many minutes before you are

rewarded. In the waiting periods you can study the topography of the

moon, for even a glass of moderate power reveals enough detail to

fascinate a space-conscious child. But sooner or later you should

begin to see the birds, lonely travelers in space glimpsed as they pass

from darkness into darkness.

In all this I have said little about identification of the birds,

insects, rocks, stars or any other of the living and nonliving things

that share this world with us. Of course it is always convenient to give a name to things that arouse our interest. But that is a separate problem, and one that can be solved by any parent who has a reasonably observant eye and the price of the various excellent handbooks that are available in quite inexpensive editions.

I think the value of the game of identification depends on how you play it. If it becomes an end in itself I count it of little use. It is possible to compile extensive lists of creatures seen and identified without ever once having caught a breath-taking glimpse of the wonder of life. If a child asked me a question that suggested even a faint awareness of the mystery behind the arrival of a migrant sandpiper on the beach of an August morning, I would be far more pleased than by the mere fact that he knew it was a sandpiper and not a plover.

W hat is the value of preserving and strengthening this sense of awe and wonder, this recognition of something beyond the boundaries of human existence? Is the exploration of the natural world just a pleasant way to pass the golden hours of childhood or is there something deeper?

I am sure there is something much deeper, something lasting and significant. Those who dwell, as scientists or laymen, among the beauties and mysteries of the earth are never alone or weary of life. Whatever the vexations or concerns of their personal lives, their thoughts can find paths that lead to inner contentment and to renewed excitement in living. Those who contemplate the beauty of the earth find reserves of strength that will endure as long as life lasts. There is symbolic as well as actual beauty in the migration of the birds, the ebb and flow of the tides, the folded bud ready for the spring. There is something infinitely healing in the repeated refrains

of nature—the assurance that dawn comes after night, and spring

after the winter.

I like to remember the distinguished Swedish oceanographer,

Otto Pettersson, who died a few years ago at the age of ninety-three,

in full possession of his keen mental powers. His son, also world-

famous in oceanography, has related in a recent book how intensely

his father enjoyed every new experience, every new discovery con-

cerning the world about him.

"He was an incurable romantic," the son wrote, "intensely in

love with life and with the mysteries of the cosmos." When he realized

he had not much longer to enjoy the earthly scene, Otto Pettersson

said to his son: "What will sustain me in my last moments is an

infinite curiosity as to what is to follow."

*I*n my mail recently was a letter that bore eloquent testimony to the lifelong durability of a sense of wonder. It came from a reader who asked advice on choosing a seacoast spot for a vacation, a place wild enough that she might spend her days roaming beaches unspoiled by civilization, exploring that world that is old but ever new.

Regretfully she excluded the rugged northern shores. She had loved the shore all her life, she said, but climbing over the rocks of Maine might be difficult, for an eighty-ninth birthday would soon arrive. As I put down her letter I was warmed by the fires of wonder and amazement that still burned brightly in her youthful mind and spirit, just as they must have done fourscore years ago.

The lasting pleasures of contact with the natural world are not reserved for scientists but are available to anyone who will place himself under the influence of earth, sea and sky and their amazing life.

Acknowledgments

This project was inspired by the spirit of Rachel Carson. I found an old copy of *The Sense of Wonder* and knew before I finished reading it that I had to produce a set of photographs for a new edition. Carson's message and the encouragement of the following people was what kept me going. My gratitude goes to all of them. ❧ Heartfelt thanks to Fran Collin. She acted as my agent and mentor. Her professionalism made this book happen. ❧ Our editor at HarperCollins, Joseph Montebello, encouraged designer Lia Calhoun and myself to have a vision and follow it. When we needed to be reined in he did so with his signature charm and grace. ❧ Associate editor Beth Bortz shared her smile, good taste and attention for detail. ❧ Fred Walter gave me his friendship and encouragement. Right from the start he knew how important this book was. ❧ Mary and Howard Phipps generously shared their property and home, which allowed me to shoot some of my favorite photographs. ❧ The publication of Linda Lear's definitive biography, *Rachel Carson: Witness for Nature*, could not have been timed better. Linda's words and kindness made me appreciate more than ever what a privilege this project was. ❧ Lia Calhoun always gave more than she was asked to give. Her elegance is a joy to everyone around her. ❧ Bill Welsh of the Boothbay Region Land Trust shared with me an unforgettable day of hiking and tide-pooling. Carson's love for the coast lives in the BRLT's mission of protecting islands and areas of Maine shoreline as reflected by the Rachel Carson Coastal Greenway. ❧ The rangers at Acadia National Park—especially Heidi Doss—have always given selflessly to my family. ❧ My good friend, Dr. William H. Klein, died during the production of this book. He was the most wonderful combination of scientist, friend and child. On more than a few occasions I looked through my viewfinder and said to myself, "Bill Klein is loving this." ❧ Once again everyone at Kelsh Wilson *design inc.* had to put up with my insecurities and tunnel vision. I thank you for your patience. ❧ Special thanks to Kevin Monko, Marsha Kear, Evan, Jeff and Debbie Morgan, Jonathan and Sam Conant, Preston Williams, Robin and Skylar Walter, Sheila Wilensky-Lanford of Oz Books, Bud Mills and everyone at Professional Color, Liz Sullivan, Marta Hallett and M.S. Wyeth, Jr. ❧ And, finally, my wife, Liz Williams, shares with me a son, Cotten, and the state of Maine. Our happiest annual moment is when we pull out of the driveway at 4 AM, point the car north to Somesville and there renew our sense of wonder for the world and each other.

Nick Kelsh

December 1997